Your One *Wild*
and *Precious* Life

Your One *Wild* and *Precious* Life

Thoughts on Vocation

MARK-DAVID JANUS, CSP, PhD

Paulist Press
New York / Mahwah, NJ

Cover image by MyStocks/Shutterstock.com
Cover and book design by Lynn Else

Library of Congress Control Number: 2018948416

ISBN 978-0-8091-5420-3 (paperback)
ISBN 978-1-58768-800-3 (e-book)

Published by Paulist Press
997 Macarthur Boulevard
Mahwah, New Jersey 07430

www.paulistpress.com

Printed and bound in the
United States of America

This book is dedicated to
Isaac Thomas Hecker and his friends, my Paulist brothers.

Who made the world?
Who made the swan, and the black bear?
Who made the grasshopper?
This grasshopper, I mean—
the one who has flung herself out of the grass,
the one who is eating sugar out of my hand,
who is moving her jaws back and forth instead of
up and down—
who is gazing around with her enormous and
complicated eyes.
Now she lifts her pale forearms and thoroughly
washes her face.
Now she snaps her wings open, and floats away.
I don't know exactly what a prayer is.
I do know how to pay attention, how to fall down
into the grass, how to kneel down in the grass,
how to be idle and blessed, how to stroll through
the fields,
which is what I have been doing all day.
Tell me, what else should I have done?
Doesn't everything die at last, and too soon?
Tell me, what is it you plan to do
with your one wild and precious life?

"The Summer Day"
Mary Oliver

CONTENTS

Introduction ix

1. Don't Be a Pagan 1

2. Fearfully and Wonderfully Made 4

3. Let God Love You 7

4. Evolutionary You 10

5. Love Begets Love 13

6. Curiosity 16

7. The Genetics of Vocation 19

8. Genetics Is Not Everything 22

9. On Not Taking Your Own Advice 24

10. The Importance of Vice 28

11. Opportunity Knocks 31

12. The Violent Bear It Away 33

13. I Am Who I Am: Vocation Out of the Closet 35

14. Jesus 38

15. *Der Heilige Geist* (The Holy Spirit) 41

CONTENTS

16. Friendship with God 44

17. The Slow Work of God 46

18. Making a Difference 49

19. Sex Is Important 51

20. Faithfulness 54

21. Running toward Love 57

22. Don't Marry a Rock 60

23. Don't Marry the Perfect Person 63

24. Holiness Is Visible 66

25. Religious Life 69

26. Thinking about Priesthood 72

27. Going to Seminary 75

28. Religious Women 78

29. Belonging 80

30. Burdens 84

31. Why Not Be a Saint? 87

32. Failure 90

33. Journey, Not Destination 93

34. God Makes It Up as We Go Along 96

If You Want to Read Some More:
Available from Paulist Press 99

INTRODUCTION

So, what are you doing with your "one wild and precious life"? The answer to this question is the mystery of vocation. Vocation: meaning what we feel we are called to do with our life, or better yet, being the person we are called to be. How we answer that question is probably the most interesting thing about us. It is how we find happiness and fulfillment. It is also how we find God.

Vocation comes from a Latin word that means calling; we are "called" to do something, we are "called" to be someone. From the Christian perspective, the one doing the "calling" is God. Since God has chosen to create the world and each one of us through the process of evolution, the divine call is also evolutionary: the call develops over time, we hear it over time, the call adapts to changes in our environment, and our response to God's call changes our environment. The responsibility for hearing, interpreting, and responding to the "call" rests with each person. No one else can answer the question of your vocation but you.

Questions about our vocation happen at various points in our lives. Initially they appear to us as daydreams, some realistic, some illusory. I wanted to be a knight at King Arthur's Round Table. Disappointed to learn this line of employment was obsolete, I had to look elsewhere. No matter, in the early stages of our life we try on potential vocations like they were clothes we are thinking of buying. Time moves on and we become more focused, choosing to develop skills we think we need or enjoy. Vocation is the process of discovery in which we learn more about ourselves, the world around us, and how we want to live in it. Eventually we pursue one path as opposed to another, but this is not the end of our story. We might become lost, or worse, bored, unsure of who we are and where we are going. When lost, it is a good idea to retrace our steps, to look afresh at ourselves, our decisions, and what excites us. Even a definitive vocational decision on our part must adapt to the changing circumstances around us. Each vocation has a life of its own, a life that demands our attention.

How to Use This Book

This is not a vocation workbook—answer these questions and you will discover whether you belong in Gryffindor or Hufflepuff. What follows is a series of reflections on various dimensions of vocation. Reading this book is like walking around a great prism, taking the time to examine the diverse dimensions light presents with each facet. Take your time as you circle the prism: don't read it all straight through. If a word or idea mirrors your life experience, circle it, scribble your thoughts about it in the margins. Take a walk and turn it over in your mind. Spend some moments in prayer with your own feelings. Ask yourself some questions you do not know the answer to. The chapter are short on purpose; only you can complete them in a way that is meaningful to you. If one chapter doesn't sing to you, move on to another—don't let yourself get stuck. Whether you are in the early days, are midway through your life, or are starting to see the end of the tunnel, each chapter is offered to provide some light as you reflect on your life, find your calling, and so enjoy your one wild, precious life.

Chapter One

DON'T BE A PAGAN

*The Fates lead the willing
and drag the unwilling.*

Seneca

When we think of what we are supposed to do with our lives, what God is calling us to be, we tend to think about our vocation as if we were pagans. We act like the ancients who believed that their lives are in the hands of the gods. The fates determine our destiny and it is up to us to figure out what their plans are for us. So we consult oracles who are supposed to have some insights into the gods. The oracles sacrifice animals and peer into the entrails for a clue as to the gods' intentions. They look at report cards, and test scores, aptitude ratings, personality characteristics, astrological signs, how fast we run one hundred meters, how much weight we can bench press, examine our reaction times, short-term memory, SAT scores, our favorite passage from Scripture, whether or not we can carry a tune, if we have any physical rhythm at all, and what shows we watch on Netflix. Gazing into these entrails, they most often tell us that the findings are unclear, but they suggest we should do this or that to clarify things. When that doesn't work out, we consult new oracles with fresh tests to apply, fresh findings to read and fresh advice for us to follow.

For Christians it goes something like this: When we die and get to heaven we will be ushered into the personnel office, where we meet the Archangel Michael. Michael reaches back into a filing cabinet, pulls out a file with our name on it, and inside the file is God's plan for our life, a plan made for us even before we were born. Placing God's file on his desk, he grabs from our hand a folder that contains the story of how we actually did with our life and lays the two side by side, and compares. We stand for an uncomfortably long time as the archangel flips through the pages, makes a few marks with a red pen, utters a heavenly sigh and an eternal grunt. When finished, he arranges his wings on either side of his chair, and leaning back, says, *"You blew it, kid. God had this whole wonderful life planned out for you."* Gesturing to the divine folder, the angel says, *"and this is what you did instead,"* tapping on the file we brought in with us. *"You started to screw it up when you were nine years old, and you made it worse every year after that."* Standing up, Michael folds a wing around our dejected shoulders, and pushing us out the door, says, *"Better luck next time."*

God does not have a secret plan for your life hidden in a heavenly filing cabinet. A vocation is about freedom, not fate. A Christian is free. The will of God in the life of a Christian is the work of the Christian and the work of God working together—both free. From a certain point of view, God is kind of making it up as he goes along: responding to our choices, our mistakes, our worries, and our desires; reacting to our quirky personality and quirkier souls.

Our vocation is God's invitation to accept the truth that God loves us and invites us to love God back. We don't guess at our vocation. We don't squeeze our lives into a predestined, preordained plan of God. We work it out with God.

We work it out in the concrete realities of the real world; work it out by living lives of faith, hope, and love in the real world. While we cannot predict what God is going do in our lives, we trust God, we trust love, and let his love be love, for us.[1] We trust the words of Jesus: *"[The Spirit] abides with you, and he will be in you. I will not leave you orphaned; I am coming to you."*

The plan for our lives is not divinely preordained. We write the plan for our lives with God.

---

1 The idea about vocation comes from a conference given by Thomas Merton, OCSO.

Chapter Two

FEARFULLY AND WONDERFULLY MADE

It was you who formed my inward parts;
you knit me together in my mother's womb.
I praise you, for I am fearfully
and wonderfully made.

Psalm 139

Just because God hasn't planned out your life from all eternity doesn't mean that God doesn't care about you or what you do. You are not an accident of evolution, a random combination of protons and neutrons. You are on purpose. You are God's purpose, and God's purpose is to love you. God loves your fingers and toes and everything in between. Your body is God's first gift to you, miraculously and wonderfully made. God intends you to enjoy it and use it; to develop its powers and abilities and use them to know God's love. The story of vocation begins with your body.

Coat hanger shoulders, narrow hipped, tall with easy grace, Dave swam the 1500-meter race, otherwise known as swimmer's hell. The 1500 meter takes so long no one cares about it. Even during swim meets, when the 1500 meter is being held fans go lunch while other swimmers nap. It is never shown on television, even during the Olympics. For this tortured race, Dave prepared twice a day, every day, leaping into a cold pool at 5:00 in the morning and again at 3:00 in the afternoon. Thousands, ten thousands of strokes, perpetual oxygen debt, swollen joints, aching ribs, hours of recovery soaking in ice baths—all of this to prepare for a race no one watches. *"When I swim I feel God's power in me,"* he told me. The pool was Dave's cathedral and each stroke his prayer of thanks to the God who knit him a body to swim. The story of your vocation begins with your body—God's first and best gift to you, given to experience God's power in you. The body is the form of the soul, so your first step is to allow your body to unfold before you (your brain is part of your body, don't forget) and marvel at what you find in front of you. Vocation begins with you cherishing your miraculous life and discovering the secret wonders God has knit within you. The Christian idea of vocation begins with the fundamental idea that God has called you to be with divine purpose. Quite a few of the meditations that follow are designed to help you reflect more deeply on yourself as God made you to be, but first things first: back to God. Do we know anything about why God made you? Indeed we do.

Once upon a time a group of earnest but confused young seekers, perhaps people not unlike yourself, traveled to the Trappist monastery in Kentucky called Gethsemane. The monks at Gethsemane abandoned everything and spent their lives in prayer seeking God. These young people went to see one monk in particular who had a reputation for being able to communicate the truths practiced within the walls of the monastery with people in the outside world. You might say that this monk was the oracle they were consulting for insight into what God has planned for their lives. They were granted an audience, and asked Fr. Louis (known in the world as Thomas Merton), *"What does a Christian have to do for salvation?"* *"Nothing,"* the monk replied. *"A Christian doesn't have to do anything to be saved. A Christian has only to believe, to believe that they are loved by God."*

Stop and think about that. You find yourself alive, wonderfully made, body and soul unfolding in grandeur before you. You are thinking about what you want to do with the life that has been given you. However, what you decide to do with your life must be rooted in the realization that you are loved. God is not objective about you, God made you to love you. You are loved into existence by a God who has given you life and a body fearfully and wonderfully made so you can experience the love that God is. The story of every vocation, the story of your vocation begins with God in love with you. Whatever you do with your life, wherever your vocation leads you, this is the place where your journey begins; this is the place to which you will always return; this is the place the devil will tempt you to forget.

Chapter Three

LET GOD LOVE YOU

Real love is about loving and letting yourself be loved.
It's harder to let yourself be loved than to love.
That is why it is so difficult to come to the
perfect love of God. We can love Him but we
must let ourselves be loved by Him.
Real love is being open to the love that comes to you.

+ Pope Francis

We have a tough time loving ourselves for free. We want to be loved because...we want to love ourselves for something...we want to deserve being loved. We want to be loved because we are the champions. Critical of ourselves as we are of others, we all wear a mask that we think is worthy of being loved, a mask behind which we hide who we really are, the person we think no one will love, the person we do not love. As compelling as this feels, and we have all felt it, this definition of love is a lie. This is the devil's theory of "earned love."

God's love for you is beyond the earned theory of love. Your vocation, the person you are and how you spend your life, will be much happier if you are to allow God to love you the way God loves you. Cardinal Walter Kasper is one of my spiritual heroes, and he describes just how God is loving you right this very moment. I am going to quote him at length here and ask you to read these words very slowly, thinking about yourself all the time. Think how you can make these words your own.

> God means precisely me—one of the billions of people on earth. Me—with the short span of life in the billions of years since the creation of the world. Me—a tiny moment, a small creature, a small flash, and a breath. Me—from a particular family with all its problems. Me—with all my minor abilities and my less minor flaws, with all the imperfections, the fragments, and the flaws in my life. Me—the one so often discouraged and sad, full of questions and some scratches, with wounds, sharp edges and corners. Me—with my questions: Who am I? Where am I, and where am I going? What is my life, what is its purpose, and in what does its happiness consist?
>
> Me—whom God has in mind from all eternity. Me, as I am—God has conceived and lovingly designed, wanted, and called Me, with body and soul and all my abilities—God has pressed me to his heart. He is crazy about me. God is after me personally, has sought me out and found me in Jesus Christ. God wanted and still wants to be my friend, and thus he died on the cross for me. To me, God has sent his Holy Spirit and has poured out his love into my heart. In God's presence, with him, I can rest easy. I am infinitely loveable for him. This gives my life worth and dignity, gives it consequence and splendor.
>
> And so I am completely unique, unrepeatable, inimitable. Without me, something would be missing

in the world; without me, the world would be poorer. Thus, I may not neglect, may not throw away, may not make a mess out of my life. On the contrary! I am valuable. And so I should, I can, I must live my life, and I must risk my life. It belongs to me. I must risk my life because God risks it with me. It was given to me. God, you have given it to me. You have given me to myself as a gift. I thank you, and I praise and glorify you for it.

Chapter Four

EVOLUTIONARY YOU

*There is no conflict between evolution
and the doctrine of the faith
regarding man and his vocation.*

St. John Paul II

*B*ack to you, and the fundamental question of vocation: Who and what has God created you to be? To do that you have to think about the process of creation. People generally think of creation in the past tense, an event that is one and done. Whether it happened in six days or with the Big Bang, creation is something God did once upon a time and is now on to other things. In the twentieth century, Catholicism decided to take evolution seriously. Evolution is not a threat to the idea that God created the world, evolution is the creative hand of God, still at work. The Dutch bishops said it best: *"If God were to remove his creative hand for an instant, everything would cease to exist."*

This has a lot to do with your vocation. First, you are the result of an evolutionary process; a lot went into making you who you are, and all that is completely out of your control. You are in a certain place in time, in a particular moment in history, in a particular place. Biologically, you are the result from a merger of an intricate number of genetic lines, and

10

now have to play with the genetic, historical, and geographic cards you are dealt. Second, you are continuing to evolve—you did not come out of the womb fully developed, ready to go; there is more work to do on you. Sigmund Freud's great insight was to take Darwin's theory of the evolution of the species and apply it to the evolution of an individual human's personality. We become who we are in response to our environment. Not only do species adapt, individual human beings adapt, change, evolve. In fact, you will only stop evolving when you pass from this life to the next. While Freud's explanations as to how this happens have become passé, medical science has affirmed his basic insight. You are, your brain is, your body is, a work in constant process. Third: you are part of God's evolutionary process. Human beings are not just the passive recipients of creation; we are part of the creative process, actors on the evolutionary stage. We used to say that we are stewards of creation, gardeners who tend and mow the Garden of Eden. We are a lot more than that: we are part of the Garden. We can bring from the world enough food and fuel to care for all, extending healthy life spans, reducing suffering, expanding diversity, exploring the universe, perhaps even making contact with other life forms. We can also plunder the earth—destroy its species, increase human and animal suffering, alter the earth's climate, even shorten its life span. What we do affects not only the evolutionary progress of human beings, we affect the evolutionary direction of the planet. We are integral parts of God's creative process.

Your vocation is part of God's evolutionary procession. There were generations beyond telling in the procession ahead of you, and now the creative hand of God is at work within you during the course of your life. You make a unique contribution to God's evolutionary process on behalf of all those who follow you. Pope Francis says, *"Although limited, human action participates in the power of God and is able to build a world adapted to the twofold corporeal and spiritual life; to build a human world for all—for all human beings, and not for a group or a privileged class."* Your vocation, whatever it turns out to be, is part of an eternal picture that deserves your awe.

Chapter Five

LOVE BEGETS LOVE

So God created humankind in his image,
in the image of God he created them;
male and female he created them.

Genesis

The story of who you are and how you got to be who you are depends on this principle: love begets love. Within the first twenty-four hours of your life, before you could even see them, the *infant* you recognized the scent of your parents. Living in a world where language did not yet have meaning, the infant you learned love by the way you were touched and tended, by the way you were soothed and excited by the sound of your parents' voices. Your first conscious movement was to locate and then gaze into your parents' eyes. The distance at which you could best focus corresponded to the distance between you nursing at your mother's breast and her eyes. As soon as you were strong enough to control the muscles in your face, you looked into her eyes and smiled at her. To respond to others with love is the image and likeness of God with which you and everybody else are made.

If vocation begins with God loving you, your vocation evolves with your ability to respond to love with love. When we talk about vocation, we often end up talking about a job, a career, a way to make a living. That's a mistake. Vocation and career may overlap, but not necessarily. Essential to a true vocation is your motivation, why you do what you choose to do, what you love, who you love, and how you love.

Governor Mario Cuomo told this story:

> I watched a small man with thick calluses on both his hands work 15 and 16 hours a day. I saw him once literally bleed from the bottoms of his feet, a man who came here uneducated, alone, unable to speak the language, who taught me all I needed to know about faith and hard work by the simple eloquence of his example. I learned about our kind of democracy from my father. And I learned about our obligation to each other from him and from my mother. They asked only for a chance to work and to make the world better for their children.

I don't think that his father saw his vocation as being a refugee and immigrant. It is unlikely he saw his vocation as working in low-paying odd jobs or his mother saw her vocation as feeding a growing family with next to nothing. It is entirely likely that they saw their vocation as being the kind of husband and wife, father and mother who would make the world a better place for their children and teach them to do the same. This couple and many like them saw their vocation as love in action.

The story of your vocation depends on an understanding that you are part of God's evolutionary creative process; it was out of love that God made you, and God made you to love in return. Made in the image and likeness of the God who is in love with you, your vocation is revealed by the way in which you mirror and transmit God's love in your life.

Father Pedro Arrupe, former Superior General of the Society of Jesus, says it this way:

> Nothing is more practical than finding God, that is, than falling in love in a quite absolute final way. What you are in love with, what seizes your imagination, will affect everything. It will decide what will get you out of bed in the morning, what you will do with your evenings, how you will spend your weekend, what you read, what you know, what breaks your heart, and what amazes you with joy and gratitude. Fall in Love, stay in love, and it will decide everything.

Chapter Six

CURIOSITY

Moses was keeping the flock of his father-in-law
Jethro, the priest of Midian; he led his flock beyond
the wilderness, and came to Horeb, the mountain of
God. There the angel of the LORD appeared to him in
a flame of fire out of a bush; he looked, and the bush
was blazing, yet it was not consumed. Then Moses
said, "I must turn aside and look at this great sight,
and see why the bush is not burned up."
When the LORD saw that he had turned aside
to see, God called to him out of the bush.

Exodus

*B*ack to thinking about you. One of the great vocational
stories in Judeo-Christian literature belongs to Moses.
Countless generations have drawn insight into their own lives
by reflecting on his life, and this is your chance.

Curiosity led Moses to God. Moses wasn't curious about
God. Moses wasn't even thinking about God. Moses was
thinking about a burning bush, wondering why it wasn't consumed by fire. In the middle of his curiosity he heard "the call"
that would change his life and the course of history. Of course,
you could say that God, knowing Moses was a curious boy,

had his angel to set the bush on fire to attract Moses, and once God got his attention he could begin speaking to him. Either way, Moses's curiosity and his willingness to act on it brought him to God.

What attracts your curiosity? What interests you? What don't you understand that you want to understand? When doing your day in and day out job, what captures your attention so completely that you leave your job behind and check it out? These are not rhetorical questions; you really need to think about this stuff, if for no other reason than that the Bible warns us that God uses our curiosity to attract our attention and begin speaking to us.

Our body is God's first gift to us, and our body is designed for curiosity. Every sensation is new for an infant, every smell, sound, sight, touch, taste an invitation to explore a world they know nothing about. It takes a baby awhile to discover that its arms and hands are its own, to move, use, grasp, wave. When a baby discovers its own legs, knees, and feet, it crawls and toddles around, exploring the world on its own. Each sensation, each new discovery, results in growth in the infant's brain and body that would not otherwise happen. Our curiosity creates us.

Curiosity is an inherent part of God's creative plan. A guiding principle in this book is that you and God work out your vocation together. Curiosity is one of the ways you do that. You are no different from Moses in that your curiosity is one of the primary ways God speaks to you. Everything you are curious about is important; it is not just curiosity about "holy" stuff. Since God created the only world you live in, there is not a "sacred world" and another separate "profane world." There is just God's world, and your curiosity about it, and the other people who live in it with you, and your curiosity about yourself.

Apathy, indifference, and fear are the enemies of curiosity, and the devil will use them all to tempt to stay away from exploring your own burning bush. Some infants learn to be fearful. Their curiosity doesn't excite them, it terrifies them. When they do not explore their environment, they do not learn, they do not grow, they do not develop their abilities, and eventually they have a tough time forming attachment to other people. The same thing happens to adults. Indifference and apathy is a lack of curiosity about other people, our own planet, and eventually, God.

If you want to discover your vocation, take a good long look at what makes you curious. Take a good long look at how you promote and encourage your curiosity. Don't be freaked out if you are not exclusively curious about "holy" things. There is not a holy world and a profane world, there is only God's world. You may be seeing God's action in ways other than those described in traditional religion. That vision may be your gift—don't talk yourself out of it.

Take a good long look at how curiosity is dampened in you and replaced by apathy and indifference. Sometimes other people throw water on your parade, and sometimes you do yourself. Everybody does it. We all talk ourselves out of a good thing. Recognize when you do it so you can guard against it.

Be warned: if, like Moses, you act on your curiosity, if you get up and go across to check out your own personal burning bush, God is likely to call your name, and nothing will ever be the same again.

Chapter Seven

THE GENETICS OF VOCATION

"Are all your sons here?" And he said, "There
remains yet the youngest, but he is keeping the sheep."
And Samuel said to Jesse, "Send and bring him; for
we will not sit down until he comes here."
He sent and brought him in. Now he was ruddy, and
had beautiful eyes, and was handsome. The LORD
said, "Rise and anoint him; for this is the one."
Then Samuel took the horn of oil, and anointed him...
and the spirit of the LORD came mightily upon
David from that day forward.

1 Samuel 16

At ten years of age, I started whacking golf balls
around the yard, over our house, and through my
parent's garage and kitchen windows. Neither their fury nor
swift retribution broke me of my need to hit golf balls. A
million balls later, I still love to practice as much as I love to
play. Nothing gives me as much release and simple pleasure
as a golf course. Rory McIlroy started playing golf when he
was just three. When he was nine years old, a year younger

than when I made my first putt, Rory was the World Under-Ten Champion. At twenty-five years of age, he won three of the most prestigious major championships and eighteen other professional tournaments. Rory McIlroy is the David of the golf world, ruddy cheeks, fine eyes, an attractive appearance, anointed king, and I am one of Jesse's leftover, unanointed, nonchampion sons.

The evolutionary process of nature gives different gifts to different people. No matter what I do and no matter how much I love golf, I will never have Rory's McIlroy's talent. The DNA fairies do not distribute their gifts equally, and while opportunity and passion play a part, the development of our abilities rest within our unique genetic parentheses. This is true even for the highly talented. Roughly 550,000 boys and 425,000 girls are good enough athletes to make the team and play high school basketball. Of that number of accomplished athletes, only 1.2 percent of girls and 1 percent of boys will go on to play NCAA Division I basketball. From that narrow group of elite players we cheer every March Madness, only 1.2 percent will be drafted to play professional basketball, which is less than .03 percent of those talented kids who played high school basketball.

My point is this: when you think about your vocation, start with an appraisal of your own abilities. What talents and abilities do you possess? The answer is not as obvious as you think. Humor me—try this exercise.

Write down five things you like about yourself; then add five things you are good at; now, put down five things that just come easy to you; write five things you have always wanted to do but never had a chance to do. Add five more things that you care deeply about—I mean you care about so deeply you are willing to sacrifice for. Not done yet: write five things you would fight for. Almost there—when Ben Platt won the Tony award for best actor in a musical for *Dear Evan Hansen*, he said, *"To all young people out there, don't waste any time trying to be like anybody else but yourself because the things that make you strange are the things that make you powerful."* Put on your list five things that make you strange.

This list doesn't add up to a job and it doesn't add up to a vocation, but it gives you some idea of what it is like to appreciate the gifts you were born with. By appreciation I don't mean resignation, I mean taking pride in who God has made you to be, pride in your talent, pride in your aspirations. You doubtless have more gifts that you are not aware of, but this is at least a place to start.

When toddlers meet one another in the sandbox, they initially keep their distance and play with the toys their mother has given them. After a while, they start looking at the toys the other toddler is playing with, and for some reason those toys always look more interesting, so one toddler grabs the other toddler's toys and a fight starts. The mothers intervene, encourage their kids to share, and when that doesn't work, try to convince them to play with their own toys. To understand your own vocation you have to learn to play with the toys God gave you to play with, the ones you naturally enjoy and are drawn to. Your vocation will use all of your toys in one way or another, so make friends with them now and don't waste your time trying to be like anybody else.

Chapter Eight

GENETICS IS NOT EVERYTHING

Saul said to David, "You are not able to go against this Philistine to fight with him; for you are just a boy, and he has been a warrior from his youth."

1 Samuel

David had no business beating Goliath. He lacked the physical ability and experience to compete. He had neither the skill nor training to be a warrior; his resume did not add up. Lacking the expected pedigree, he enjoyed no one's confidence. If David had listened to his brothers, or his father, or Saul the king, he would never have put himself forward, taken the risk, seized his destiny, and Goliath would have been the winner.

The prophet Samuel did not think much of David, so the angel of the Lord read him the riot act: *"Do not look on his appearance or on the height of his stature, because I have rejected him; for the LORD does not see as mortals see; they look on the outward appearance, but the LORD looks on the heart."* In the last meditation, I encouraged you to look at your talents and not waste your time wishing for the talents others possess. If you have a sense of your talents, now do what God does, and look at your heart. It is the heart that frees you to do what only you and God know you can do.

People will sell you short. The less you look like what they expect, the less your background and resume matches the traditional model, the more likely you are to be written off. If you are part of a "minority group," you are likely to encounter prejudice. Don't forget this: They do not know what you know; they do not see what God sees. They don't see you.

One more thing to remember: David did not kill Goliath in the conventional way. He did not use the armor or weapons Saul gave him. He defeated Goliath using the tools he knew best. David defeated Goliath his way, with his experience and talents. Saul didn't send him to defeat Goliath, God did. David and God worked out the vocation thing together.

Chapter Nine

ON NOT TAKING YOUR OWN ADVICE

But sir, how can I deliver Israel?
My clan is the weakest in Manasseh,
and I am the least in my family.

Judges

Gideon is a great vocation story. Nobody has read it, but everyone has lived it. Gideon's world is going to hell in a handbasket and Gideon is everyone's idea of a nobody. Then the angel of the LORD (code in the Bible for God) appears to him, frightening Gideon with the news that God has chosen him to fix things. Gideon is no David, eager to take on Goliath. Gideon knows he is not up to it. He is afraid. God is mistaken in choosing him for anything but an inconsequential life.

I know this sounds stupid, but we don't know ourselves, not really. I won't deny that there are parts of us we know that no one else does: thoughts, feelings, experiences, and dimensions of ourselves we never share and others never guess. People paid me good money as a clinical psychologist to talk about themselves so I could understand them. However, I never thought I knew them completely, and I never thought they told me everything. After all, there are chapters in our story we never read out loud. Not only don't others know our secrets, we don't know all of them either.

There are some simple reasons for this. First, we are pretty complicated creatures. A lifetime of experiences imprint themselves on our body and brain, making us who we are. Our earliest experiences, those that laid down the basic physical and neural tracks we spend the rest of our lives riding, happened before we have a conscious memory of them. Self-sorted, analyzed, and organized, these basic building blocks operate unconsciously, reflexively. We are no more aware of them than we are the physical processes we use when we write our name, tie our shoes, or ride a bike. The more inbred our experiences are, the more efficient we are in navigating and negotiating life.

For all the good our unconscious and reflexive processes are, they have a downside. They make up the filter we use to evaluate new experiences. We tend to like new experiences that easily fit our old patterns and tend to reject those that don't. Our gut reactions, the instincts on which we depend, can, if we are not careful, screen out new information and new experiences. As a result we stop learning, stop doing, and build ourselves a comfortable rut. This is how prejudices form within us without us knowing they are there. Our instincts feel so right, are so familiar and convincing, we don't challenge them.

The second reason it is hard for us to truly know ourselves is that we don't know what we don't know. Our experiences form us, but there are lots of experiences we haven't had a chance to enjoy. One of my German friends told me about his "gap" year, the year between high school and college Europeans typically take off to travel and take a break from studying. Burkhardt came to the United States, where, he told me, *"I learned that everything I thought was normal, what I thought everybody did, was actually just what Germans do."* Experiencing a new idea or a new experience provides us with the opportunity to expand skills we never knew we had, and to think thoughts we had never imagined. There is a neurological correlate for this. Just before adolescence, the brain has an "overproduction" of gray cells, neurons, and synapses (the connections between cells). It is as if the brain is gearing up to engage in a wide range of activities. However, if those activities or experiences don't happen, the brain cells start to be pruned away—stripping away the unused cells and focusing on those we do use. From a biological point of view, this is a matter of "use it or lose it." If we don't know we have ability we don't develop it, and if we do not develop it, we lose the capacity to do so.

This is why you need other people to help you with your vocation. No, you don't need someone to tell you what to do with your life, but you need people to help you understand that there is more to you than you think, and there is more to the world than you think. It is one thing when others sell you short; it is worse when you sell yourself short.

Father T. J. Martinez, SJ, was the powerhouse founder of Christo Rey High School in Houston, Texas. Starting with no school, no money, no donors, no teacher, no students, Fr. T. J. convinced donors in Houston to start a Jesuit high school in the poorest part of town for the most disadvantaged students in town. His goal was not that they attend school, nor that they graduate from high school. His goal was that they would attend college, each and every one of them. To do that, these students, most of them non-Catholic, would have to attend a Jesuit high school (without a football team), have a longer school day, shorter vacations, and work a day a week at a special internship to help pay for their education. His hardest task was walking the streets of East Houston to find and convince kids that they could have a future they never imagined. He had to convince them they could be successful at something at which they had only failed. He had to convince them that years of sacrifice would lead to a reward that no one in their family and no one in their neighborhood every achieved. He had to convince them not just to want it, he had to convince them to do it. As of this writing that is exactly what the students of Christo Rey have done.

The students of Christo Rey needed someone to help them see in themselves something they could not see themselves. You might need someone to help you see more of you than you can see yourself.

Chapter Ten

THE IMPORTANCE OF VICE

J was made merely in the image of God but not otherwise resembling him enough to be mistaken for him by anybody but a very near-sighted person.

Mark Twain

*B*road shouldered, powerfully built, he moves with that easy leopard-like grace possessed only by athletes or dancers. Bolt upright, intense, one leg or the other bouncing, he sat in my office discussing his possible vocation to the priesthood. He brought to our discussion his focus: the linear concentration and preparation that served him so well in his athletic career. Priesthood being a serious thing, he was ruthless in assessing its challenges and responsibilities paired against his abilities and shortcomings. If I were to guide him, direct him, coach him, he wanted to be sure that I had all his vital statistics at my disposal. *"I am very ambitious, you know, very ambitious."* Having whispered his most disqualifying secret, he leaned back into the chair to wait for my reaction.

His ambition was not a revelation. He was an NCAA Division I scholarship athlete, of course he was ambitious! As a clinical psychologist with years of assessing personality, to me his concealed ambition was palpable. I have seen it in so many good people. I know it in myself. I took a sip of water, and now it was my turn to sit upright in my chair and lean forward with my reply. *"Don't you think God knows that? Do you honestly think God doesn't know you? God may be calling you because you are ambitious. If you become a priest, God may use your ambition to advance his kingdom, and maybe God will use it to tame you."*

True, ambition is not a great attribute for priesthood; an attitude of service is much better. But God has to work with what he's got, and God has a history of calling people with one flaw or another, or likely many flaws. Remember, your vocation is result of a partnership between you and God, working together, even with your flaws. God does not restrict himself to saints, geniuses, and prodigies. There are very few of those around, and unless you are one of them, beware of the temptation to compare your shortcomings with the dazzling success of others. God made you, God calls you to live life to the full, and your own setbacks are no excuse for not answering the call.

I have been hearing confessions for a long time, and my experience is that Catholics are not, by and large, Renaissance sinners. We are specialists: we find one or two sins we really like, and we get good at them. They might morph a bit over time, but generally, like barnacles they stay attached to the ship. Oh, there are saints who scrape all the barnacles off. People do change, some temptations lose their attraction. But for the rest of us, their allure remains irresistible. Even Pope Francis, to the disquiet of many, describes himself as "a sinner." Understanding yourself as a sinner is not an exercise in self-hatred, it is the first step in allowing yourself to be saved by the crucified Lord. What I mean is this: the man sitting in my office at the beginning of this chapter was thoughtful, self-reflective, and self-critical. Those are all positive attributes—providing you share them with God and do not become absorbed in self-hatred or the prideful expectation that you too can be a god. Anselm Grün, a Benedictine monk, gives us an idea of how God works with self-criticism and transforms it into something useful: *"We must let go of the illusion that we are only spiritual, only loving, only in control of ourselves and free. We are at the same time godless, empty, aggressive, out of control, and inwardly captive. This journey succeeds only if we make it as a way of the cross."*

The point is this, you may never overcome your negative attributes; your vices may always live with your virtues, forming a cross you will carry your entire life. The way of the cross is not simply the experience at Calvary two thousand years ago; it is the experience of your own contradictions seeking to put to death the love within you. If you pursue your vocation honestly and courageously, you will not carry your cross alone. The Risen Lord will carry it with you.

Chapter Eleven

OPPORTUNITY KNOCKS

*Then Joshua son of Nun sent two men secretly from
Shittim as spies, saying, "Go, view the land, especially
Jericho." So they went, and entered the house of a
prostitute whose name was Rahab, and spent the night
there. The king of Jericho was told, "Some Israelites
have come here tonight to search out the land." Then
the king of Jericho sent orders to Rahab, "Bring
out the men who have come to you, who entered your
house, for they have come only to search out the whole
land." But the woman took the two men and hid them.
Then she said, "True, the men came to me, but I
did not know where they came from. And when it
was time to close the gate at dark, the men went out.
Where the men went I do not know. Pursue them
quickly, for you can overtake them."*

Joshua

We talk about vocation as if it is the result of a deliberate
discernment process, undertaken at our own pace, in
our own time and in our own way. It happens at a predictable
point in our life, with an array of choices before us. It grows

organically from within, consistent with our life, personality, and habits. The story of Rahab reminds us it doesn't always happen that way. Sometimes opportunity knocks.

She was plying her trade when well-informed police come to the door, demanding she hand over the spies who visited her in the night before. Quickly, she lies to the guards, hides her customers on her roof till dark, and helps them escape by night, all at considerable risk to herself. Given her profession, we cannot call her an observant Jew, but she was a keen observer of these men and their God. Overnight she comes to believe in God more than they do; actually she always did. Rahab strikes a bargain to save her life and the life of her family by saving the lives of her spies. She has no idea whether they are going to keep their word and save her in return; men who visit brothels are not famously honest. She saves them all the same. We don't think of prostitutes as saviors, but God appears to be able to call on everyone.

I imagine that not everyone who hid Jews from Nazis or participated in the Underground Railroad, or who fights for equality for minorities, or who struggles against Boko Haram or ISIS are conventional saints. During the terrorist bombing in Manchester, England, a homeless man who had been living rough on the streets ran into danger to help while everyone else ran out to safety. In the recent Texas floods, plenty of sinners risked their lives to help people they did not know, while more than one churchgoing Christian remained warm and dry. Not everyone who raises a family, or struggles alone, does so with a halo.

She acted on the spur of the moment. She acted when she was in danger. No angels came to warn or encourage her. All on her own, she saw the right thing to do and she did it.

A sage, salty Paulist priest named Fr. Joe Gallagher was fond of saying, *"Never resist a good impulse."* It just may be how you find your vocation, even when you aren't looking for it.

Chapter Twelve

THE VIOLENT BEAR IT AWAY

*From the days of John the Baptist until now
the kingdom of heaven has suffered violence,
and the violent take it by force.*

Jesus

Kamel, a fifteen-year-old Syrian refugee boy, was interviewed by the BBC. *"I used to want to grow up and be a footballer and play for Real Madrid,[2] but now I work so I can provide for my family."* He works in a Turkish shoe factory in Gaziantap, southern Turkey. He and his younger brother work twelve hours a day, six days a week, and together earn eighty-four dollars. If he does not work, he cannot stay in Turkey. If he does not work, his family does not survive. Twelve-year old Hussein works in the same village with dangerous heavy machinery, making fifty dollars per week; he too is the sole support of his family.

Violence and greed has stolen the vocations of these Syrian boys and so many like them in the war torn Middle East. They are not alone. Throughout the world, ignorance

---

2 A very popular football (soccer) club in Spain.

and misogyny under the guise of tradition prevents girls from receiving an education and women equal rights. In the United States, racism denies equal opportunity in education and employment to African Americans. Irrational fear of the other people allows immigration to break up the families of migrant workers under the righteous ruse that we are protecting our borders from people not so unlike Kamel and Hussein, people doing work no one else wants, at wages no one can afford, simply so their families will not starve. Economic disparity prevents increasing numbers of people from gaining access to the higher education necessary to find independence. Without that education, vocations and hopes are squandered.

To achieve your vocation, you may have to struggle against the people of violence Jesus predicts you will find. When they do find you and attempt to wrestle your vocation away, attempt to deny you the opportunity to do or to be the person God made you to be, you must defy them. Vocation is worth fighting for.

What will happen to Kamel and Hussein? Will they survive the war? Will they live? Will they be able to earn enough to support their families? Will they ever be able to return to school and football pitch to pursue their dreams and discover their vocation? Will people of violence take them by storm? Will people of violence take you by storm?

Chapter Thirteen

I AM WHO I AM

Vocation Out of the Closet

*"O my Lord, you only are our king; help me, who am
alone and have no helper but you, for my danger is in
my hand....Remember, O Lord; make yourself known
in this time of our affliction, and give me courage....
Put eloquent speech in my mouth before the lion, and
turn his heart to hate the man who is fighting against
us, so that there may be an end of him and those
who agree with him. But save us by your hand, and
help me, who am alone and have no helper but you,
O Lord....O God, whose might is over all, hear the
voice of the despairing, and save us from the hands of
evildoers. And save me from my fear!"*

Prayer of Queen Esther

When we finally decide on a vocation, we think we
will do so to great applause. Friends, family, and
the world are eagerly waiting our decision and future success.
While I hope that is true for you, I have to remind you that
arriving at your vocation can be dangerous.

The Book of Esther is, as you might suspect, about a woman named Esther, a Jew living in exile. The Persian king Ahasuerus and his queen Vashti had a fight that prompted the king to look for an addition to his harem to be a new, less contentious queen. Among the beautiful virgins brought to his palace was Esther, and she won the beauty pageant, becoming queen of the most powerful empire in the world. Hers was not a bad vocation if you can swing it, which she did with the advice of her Uncle Mordecai, who told her it was best to keep the part about her being a Jew secret. It was a small price to pay for being queen. Time passed and everything was going well; it was good to be queen. One day, King Ahasuerus's chief advisor told him the captured Jews were not assimilating properly—meaning that although defeated and captured, they were still being Jews. They were not blending into the Persian melting pot. The obvious answer was to slaughter them all and keep all their money, and the king consented that some preemptive homeland security was necessary.

Queen Esther, presiding in the harem, is unaware of any of this until Mordecai contrives to get a note passed to her, asking her to intercede with her husband the king. Queen Esther no longer lives with Jews, and is not likely to ever have anything to do with them again. If she comes out to the king as a Jew, she risks not only her vocation as queen, she risks her life. There is no guarantee that anything will happen except she dies with everyone else, and the king will once more look for a new queen. She turns to prayer to figure out whether her vocation as queen is more important than her vocation to be herself. It is interesting to me that she does not pray for God to fix everything. She prays that God give her courage, that God give her the ability to be persuasive, that God give her the wisdom to outmaneuver the king's top advisor. She prays that God help her with her own fear.

Long story short, she decides if she is going to be queen, she will be queen just as she is. She is not going to hide anymore. Esther finds the courage to come out to the king and convince him that the real threat to his throne is the prejudice of his advisors. The happy ending: Queen Esther stays queen, no longer hides in the closet, and her people, the Jews, are saved and the prejudiced are punished.

Conflicts occur between the demands of your vocation, how people expect you to carry out your vocation, and who you are. This conflict between who you are and the role you play in society does not always end happily, not even in the Bible (see the story of the Maccabees). When you experience the conflict between the expectations people have about your vocation and who you know you are, remember Esther. Pray for courage, pray for eloquence, pray for wisdom, pray that God saves you from the fear of being yourself.

Chapter Fourteen

JESUS

Softly and tenderly Jesus is calling—
Calling for you and for me;
Patiently Jesus is waiting and watching—
Watching for you and for me![3]

Jesus was a Jew of the first third of the first century. He didn't know anything about global warming, never imagined nuclear war, and had no idea that the Americas existed. He knew nothing about investment banking, or computer technology. He knew nothing about contemporary religious life for men and women, and could not give you the job description of a parish priest. He lived before women's suffrage, gender identity, and the myriad questions that surround health care. Although Jesus has precious little advice to give you on the specifics of whatever vocation you and God are working out together, he is the place where your vocation begins and the touchstone to which you must return long after your vocation is decided.

In his one wild and precious life, Jesus teaches us who the God of love is, and what it means to love in return. Whatever form your specific vocation takes, the overarching Christian vocation is to follow Jesus. While Jesus of Nazareth

---

3 Traditional American hymn.

never dreamed of your complicated modern life, the Risen Lord Jesus is eager to accompany you on a journey to the life of love that does not end. Jesus is not going to barge into your life and take possession of your soul. He waits for your invitation to form a friendship. The first followers of Jesus were called "people of the way," a poetry that suggests we choose to make our way through life alongside Jesus.

So how do you issue the invitation for Jesus to join you? My best advice is this: read his story told in the Gospels (Matthew, Mark, Luke, and John). Read Jesus's story again and again. The Gospel stories are not all the same. Each is told from a slightly different perspective, at a different point in time, and in different circumstances. Read them all, but discover your favorite Gospel. Turn Jesus's words and deeds over in your soul; do your best to understand his thinking; see the world and yourself through his eyes. Allow his blood to flow in your veins, allow your heart to beat in rhythm with his. While the decisions are always yours, you do not have to find your vocation all on your own. The Risen Christ, as you come to know him in the Gospels will provide you with just enough light to make your own way, taking one step and then another.

There are some words I find myself going back to again and again. Let me share them with you:[4]

> *Following Jesus does not mean slavishly copying*
> *His life.*
> *It means making his choice of life your own*
> *Starting from your own potential*
> *And in the place where you find yourself.*
> *It means living for the values*
> *For which Jesus lived*

---

4 Rule for a New Brother.

And died.
It means following the path He took
And seeing things as He saw them.
If there is anything in which this life,
This way, can be expressed
In which God has revealed himself most clearly,
It is the reality of love.
You are someone
Only insofar as you are love
And only what has turned to love in your life
Will be preserved.
He is the one who has loved most!
He will teach you to put the center of yourself
Outside.
For no one has greater love
Than one who dies for his friends...
So keep Jesus Christ before your eyes.
Don't hesitate to go anywhere He leads you;
Don't stay where you are and don't look back,
But look forward with eagerness to what lies
*   ahead.*

Chapter Fifteen

DER HEILIGE GEIST
(THE HOLY SPIRIT)

The wind blows where it chooses, and you hear
the sound of it, but you do not know where
it comes from or where it goes.
So it is with everyone who is born of the Spirit.

Jesus

Just like the way it sounds in German, *Der Heilige Geist*. *Geist*, meaning the ghost, spirit, breath, the essence of a thing, or person. Your spirit is who you are that makes you different from anyone else. It is more than your personality or talents or weaknesses. The fire in your soul is your spirit. The Holy Spirit is the fire of God's "soul," if we want to stretch the analogy. God's Spirit hovered over the formless void and creation came forth—the Big Bang! God's Spirit brought Jesus into life, infused his teaching and miracles, raised him from the dead. Jesus breathed his Spirit on his followers and they were "born again," as it were, made fresh with God's Spirit within them.

Geists, Spirits, are insubstantial but nevertheless real. There are times we cannot quite put our finger on what makes us who we are. We may not be able to describe ourselves to others but we know when we are real. Like Jesus's analogy of the wind, we are not always sure where we are coming from or where we are going, but we can feel when we are authentic, we can feel when we belong, we can feel when we are doing what we know we must do—because of who we are. We can hear, even if no one else can, the unique sound that only we can make, the sound of our soul. Your vocation is the sound of your soul.

Dear Evan Hansen begins with the hero singing,

> *When you're falling in a forest and there's nobody*
> *around*
> *Do you ever really crash, or even make a sound?*
> *Did I ever make a sound?*
> *Did I ever make a sound?*
> *It's like I never made a sound*
> *Will I ever make a sound?*

The Holy Spirit works alongside your spirit, encouraging you to create and perform your own sound, the sound that is your vocation. Your spiritual life is the attention you pay to listening to your spirit, listening to God's Spirit within you. Your vocation is how you and God make your sound heard.

Make some time to listen to yourself. Some people need to be alone and quiet and reflective to hear themselves and attend to the Holy Spirit. Other people need to be active, engaged, moving, in discussion with others to hear themselves think and hear God speak. However you do it is fine, but be intentional about yourself, be intentional about God. You know that you are on the right track when you find some resonance with these words from my friend, Fr. Tolentino: "*When we think of the Holy Spirit of God, we think of something that comes down upon us and is combined with that which we are. It is in us. In other words, it is in me and what I am. This outpouring or effusion, as the word effusion indicates, is a kind of fusion. And I feel that God in me makes me to be, gives me courage for the battle, wisdom for the word, joy for the dance."*

Chapter Sixteen

FRIENDSHIP WITH GOD

The Glory of God is the human person fully alive.

St. Irenaeus

common theme in Christian spirituality is that God sends disasters, trials, and tribulations to test the courage and faithfulness of his friends. That is how the author of the Book of Genesis explained Abraham going off to sacrifice his son Isaac, and the author of the Book of Job used the same explanation for Job's suffering. That same piety has crept into vocational spirituality from time to time. To read some biographies of saints you think they were never happier than when they were miserable. If a vocation includes trial, deprivation, and acute pain, God is happy with you.

God does not work that way. The God Jesus calls Father does not plan a vocation of suffering for anyone. In the Gospel of John, Jesus says, *"I came that they may have life, and have it abundantly"* and again, *"I have said these things to you so that my joy may be in you, and that your joy may be complete."* That doesn't sound like a vindictive pagan god to me. A priest friend of mine in Portugal, Fr. Tolentino Mendonça, comes at it from a different slant: he suggests that we see our vocation not as a test from God but rather as friendship with

God. As our friend, God desires only what is best for us. Fr. Tolentino says it this way:

> Our humanity tells God's story: our face tells us how his face is; our hands let us see his; he speaks in our words, and the more open our gestures are, the better he breathes; our eyes reveal how his eyes sparkle; our silences and our laughter are maps for those who wish to reach him. Our frailty reaches the power of his compassion. The absences in which we lose ourselves make it possible to perceive ever more clearly his friendship. Like any mother or father, he does not want his son or daughter to be taller or shorter, fair or dark. All he wants is for his children to be what they are to the full. There is nothing in us that is either unknown or indifferent to him: interruptions and new beginnings, frustrations and challenges, times of turbulence and tranquility. He arrives at all hours, without ever going away. He enters when we open the door to him, but he is always there present. He is here and he is there. He is embracing us now and at the same time, he is waiting to enfold us in the embrace without end.

All God wants is for you to be who you are to the full. Being who you are is going to test your resolve. Lots of people will insist that you be as they want you to be. There will be plenty of hardship, suffering, and pain involved as you strive to be yourself with integrity. The good news is that when you try to be yourself, and people make that hard to do, your friend God stands by you.

Chapter Seventeen

THE SLOW WORK OF GOD

Above all, trust in the slow work of God.
We are quite naturally impatient in everything
to reach the end without delay.
We would like to skip the intermediate stages;
we are impatient of being on the way to something
unknown, something new...and so
I think it is with you,
your ideas mature gradually—let them grow,
let them shape themselves without undue haste.
Don't try to force them on....
Only God could say what this new spirit gradually
forming within you will be.
Give our Lord the benefit of believing
that his hand is leading you,
and accept the anxiety of feeling yourself
in suspense and incomplete.

Pierre Teilhard de Chardin

Deciding what to do with your life is different from
deciding between green beans and yellow beans,
between hamburgers or hot dogs. Your vocation is not an

either-or decision. Knowing what you want, even what you like, may not be as easy as it sounds. You might change your mind. Deciding on who you are and how you are going to go about being you, may take a long time, longer than other people expect, longer than you expect. Why is it so hard for you to figure yourself out? The delay may be due to God.

Remember, a vocation is a partnership, two free wills—you and God—working together and it may just be that God is not finished with you yet. God's creative process did not stop when sperm met egg and you appeared; God's creative process in your life is ongoing. Jeremiah the prophet likened a vocation to the relationship between a potter and the clay on the spinning wheel. The potter forms and reforms the spinning clay, and only in time is the ultimate shape and form revealed: the final result a surprise, even for the potter.

What you feel as indecision may be your own process of growth, your personal evolution not yet at the point where you can feel definite about an ultimate choice. Like tectonic plates moving slowly beneath the surface of the earth, you may not yet have settled in your final position.

None of this takes into account the changing world around us. Vocations do not exist in a vacuum; they exist in a rapidly changing world. An average baby boomer, who inherited a relatively stable world, held about 11.9 jobs between the ages of eighteen and fifty.[5] I am an example. I am a baby boomer and became a priest, which you would think to be a relatively stable vocation. I can think of no less than nine completely distinct types of jobs I have held as a priest. The church I currently serve is completely different from the one I was prepared to serve. No one will even hazard a guess as to how volatile and varied the millennial job market will be,

---

5 US Department of Labor, August 24, 2017; USDL17-1158.

much less what different forms your world will take. Not only are you unsettled, the world around you is unsettled.

Don't be impatient with yourself. Give yourself the time you need. You deserve it. You are not in this all by yourself. Trust the slow will of God. Have confidence that each shifting step you take, you take with God, and God will accompany you to your ultimate destination, however long that takes.

Chapter Eighteen

MAKING A DIFFERENCE

Give me the grace dear God, to see the bareness
and misery of the places where you are
not adored but desecrated.

Flannery O'Connor

$\mathcal{F}$ ollowing Jesus will lead you directly to people to whom life is not kind. They suffer from poverty, discrimination, and disease. They suffer from natural disasters and disasters cruelly inflicted by human beings. Some are the intended victims of evil people, while others are the collateral damage of circumstances beyond anyone's control. There are also people who are suffering because of their own actions. They were stupid. They were selfish. They were reckless. The only thing that matters is this: the Risen Lord Jesus loves them all. He identifies with them, so much so that Jesus says, *"Just as you did it to one of the least of these who are members of my family, you did it to me....Truly I tell you, just as you did not do it to one of the least of these, you did not do it to me."*

Whatever your vocation leads you, if you are a follower of Jesus, somewhere, somehow, it will lead you to make a difference in the lives of people who suffer. Not everyone is Mother Teresa, directly serving the poorest of the poor. You may be more like a Bill Gates, who after a career of making

Microsoft is now devoted to the poorest of the poor, striving to eliminate illness and creating educational opportunities. Not everyone is Bill Gates either. Most of us are somewhere in between Mother Teresa and the Bill and Melinda Gates Foundation. No matter your vocation, people in need will have a place of privilege in your life, not as a matter of political correctness, but because a vocation worked out with God leads you to see people as God sees people. You will see the person in need as your neighbor, and your Good Samaritan soul will not let you rest until you reach out to them with help that feels like help.

If God is calling you to anything, God is calling you to love. Pope Francis puts love in perspective when he says, *"To love is to have the capacity to shake a dirty hand and the capacity to look into the eyes of those in a situation of degradation and say: 'For me you are Jesus.'"* So whatever your vocation, find a dirty hand to shake, find someone everyone ignores or some people hate, find someone who has more needs than you can possibly meet, and somehow, someway, with words or without, let them know they are Jesus to you.

Chapter Nineteen

SEX IS IMPORTANT

Let him kiss me with the kisses of his mouth!
For your love is better than wine,
your anointing oils are fragrant,
your name is perfume poured out;
therefore the maidens love you.

Song of Solomon

There are those who believe God only invented sex because he couldn't think of any other way for humans to reproduce. The idea of people splitting in two like an amoeba is too unsettling to think about. Consequently, we are resigned to sexual reproduction as a necessary evil, indulged only when compulsory. Sexual thoughts, sexual desire, sexual arousal are examples of evolution gone off the rails. Church Lady, from *Saturday Night Live*, doubtless would call them tools of Satan!

Your sexuality is an important part of your thinking about vocation because it is an important part of you. Sexuality is not defined by the design of your genitals. Sexuality begins in the brain and works its way downward toward the genitalia and outward to the senses. Your brain is the primary sexual organ that makes sexual urges possible and controls them, defines objects of arousal, catalogues and retrieves stimulating experiences and memories, originates and mediates sexual behaviors, and creates meaning for sexual experience. Your sexuality includes desire, arousal, and an understanding of the social customs that surround whatever gender you are. Your sexuality extends beyond sexual arousal, desires, and actions to the expectation of how men and women are supposed to act in situations that have nothing to do with sexual arousal or desire. A twenty-first-century understanding sees vocation as an expression of your sexuality, not as a rejection or escape from it. Why would you want to escape from one of the most intimate gifts God has given you?

At the most basic level, your sexual desires move you out of yourself toward others. Remember the first time you felt yourself wanting to just look at someone? To hear the sound of their voice? Remember wanting to be next to them, wanting to think of something to say to them, hoping they will say something back; wanting to hold their hand—and then, as Romeo said to Juliet, to *"let lips do what hands do; they pray, grant thou, lest faith turn to despair"*? That first kiss, that first crush, and all those that follow remind you that you are not made to be alone, but are made to be in relationship to others. Sexual desire is not the product of anthropomorphized sperms and eggs operating under the direction of genes functioning like little biological generals plotting their campaign to survive to the next generation. Sexual desires remind you that selfishness is not enough, you were made for a life of mutual love, life-giving love, everlasting love.

For most, this desire finds its best expression in marriage. I especially like the marriage rite from old Book of Common Prayer: *"With this ring, I thee wed, with my body, I thee worship."* The integration of sexuality and spirituality in a covenant of life and love is the ultimate form of chastity. The rest of us will find a different way to integrate our sexuality and spirituality. We will give ourselves in relationship in a different style: in service to country, the human community, or environment; perhaps in a celibate commitment to ministry or religious community. If this form of relationship is your vocation, it must be so because it expresses your sexuality, not because it negates it.

Sex is important in understanding and living your vocation. At its most basic level, sexual desire reminds you that you are created to move outside of yourself toward others. At its ultimate expression, you will give your partner all that you have and all that you are and you will allow yourself to be gifted with all your partner is. In this mutual exchange you will be mirroring the love of Christ. For others, the celibate expression of your sexuality will be your ultimate gift. Married, single, celibate, God seasons your love forever with your sexuality.

Chapter Twenty

FAITHFULNESS

Where you go, I will go;
where you lodge, I will lodge;
your people shall be my people,
and your God my God.

Book of Ruth

Where you go, I will go. These are not words exchanged between lovers, they are words Ruth promises her recently widowed and aged mother-in-law. Go start over, the old woman says, find a husband, be happy. Start a new life; there is no future for you here. Ruth tells her no, she will hang in with her. She will not leave because prospects are bleak. In the face of disaster, Ruth increases her commitment to the old woman, and together these women give us an insight into God. We say that we are made in the image and likeness of God, our faithfulness is how we mirror God's image. God is nothing if not faithful. The entire Hebrew Scriptures are the record of God's faithfulness to people who are not faithful back. Jesus is the ultimate New Testament demonstration of God's faithfulness, faithful even to the people who put him to death: *"No one has greater love than this, to lay down one's life for one's friends."*

Our fundamental vocation is to be faithful. To be where

we said we would be. To do what we said we were going to do. You can expect me to stand by you, because I am your friend: your friend in good times and in bad, in sickness and in health. Win or lose, you can trust me.

The best translation of the Greek word St. Paul uses for faith is the English word *trust*. To be a person of faith is to be a person of trust. To believe in God is to trust in God. To be a faithful person is to be a trustworthy person. So what does this have to do with your vocation?

Your vocation is to trust God. A rabbi once told me, *"Abram did not believe in God, Abram believed God."* He trusted God enough to do what God asked. So don't believe in God as an interesting or possible idea, but trust God enough to do what the Spirit of God calls you to do. This sounds so very pious, *"Believe God, trust God, be faithful to God"*; it sounds like a religious bumper sticker. Trite as it sounds, you simply cannot be faithful to your vocation, whatever it is, without first developing a faithful relationship to God. In every vocation, you are going to run across two major obstacles: yourself and other people. In every vocation are responsibilities, obstacles, and difficulties that bring out the worst in us. We don't like the worst in us. Laziness, greed, envy, jealousy, frustration, lack of appreciation, lack of talent, failure: these do not look good on us and we don't like ourselves when we feel this way. The obvious answer is to quit—go somewhere else, with someone else, and do something else. Anything is better than coming face-to-face with my inadequacy. I don't just experience laziness, greed, envy, jealousy, frustration, lack of appreciation, lack of talent, or failure in myself, I experience it in other people. If I cannot run away from myself, I certainly can run away from them. I have only one wild and precious life to live, why spend it being Sisyphus pushing the same rock up the same hill every day?

The act of being faithful to your vocation in spite of difficulties shapes you, hones you, maximizes your talents, develops new capacities, and increases the likelihood that you will be the person you were always meant to be. This is where the idea of friendship with God is powerful. Trusting God's friendship helps you be faithful to yourself and others. Again, from my friend Fr. Tolentino:

> God himself is the reason why we must love God and love one another. Our feelings often stand in the way of our living in friendship because we love as a function of the things that happen to please us....It is by uniting ourselves with God that we overcome the ties and equivocations that interiorly make us unable to go further in our search for truth. By getting close to the inner friend who is God himself, we receive from him the love that enables us to love our friends in the right way.

Chapter Twenty-One

RUNNING TOWARD LOVE

David danced before the LORD with all his might...
leaping and dancing before the LORD.

2 Samuel

t the risk of sounding stupid, let me remind you that you should enjoy your vocation. You should enjoy the person that you are. I mention it because there are spiritualities out there that feature pain and suffering, as if God was happy only when people are miserable. Don't believe it. There is plenty of suffering in the world; God does not want you to add to it. Jesus said, *"I have said these things to you so that my joy may be in you, and that your joy may be complete."* Those are not the words of a man pushing misery. Those are the words of someone who is pushing us to love with all our heart, soul, mind, and body. Those are the words of someone who wants us to love ourselves and love others the same way. Your vocation, whatever it is, should make you happy. Maybe not every minute of every day—most things involve a certain amount of sacrifice to achieve, and there are boring moments in life—but overall, your vocation should bring you happiness. *"From silly devotions and sour-faced saints, Lord deliver us!"* St. Teresa of Avila used to say.

An interesting thing about happiness is that it is a derivative emotion. There is no happiness button you push; you find yourself happy because of something you do, a job well done, a relationship with someone, or with your surroundings, relishing something beautiful, exciting, a person, an environment, an idea even. Happiness comes from engagement, and it can be found even in times of trial. *"Joy is a gift that pays me surprise visits,"* Fr. Tolentino reminds us.

The happiness that accompanies your vocation is not a prosperity gospel preaching that God intends for you to be rich, healthy, and prosperous. This happiness comes from love that is given. I wish I could remember the name of the program; it made a big impression on me. It was a "reality show" about a girl obsessed with fashion. She saw her future as a successful designer. In this scenario she was sent to India, where the clothes she hoped to design were made. She went to work in one of the sweatshops where clothes are sown, and lived with a poor Indian family in their two-room hut with dirt floors. Initially aghast at the appalling conditions in which she had to work and live, she learned a few things about herself: she learned that she hadn't been a very good daughter, sister, or friend. The overworked and impoverished family with whom she was forced to live exhibited more love and happiness between themselves than she experienced in her own family, mostly, she decided, because she had been too self-absorbed and selfish to know and love her own family. I thought she was awfully brave to allow herself to come to that realization, brave enough to find happiness. Joy requires a certain amount of bravery, for joy is born when we open our life, when we open our heart and take the time to make others comfortable. When we invite people into our life, we never know what they will bring with them.

David is one of the most interesting of all biblical figures. Shepherd boy, warrior, king, sinner, saint, and songwriter. He experienced a good deal of tragedy in his life, and caused a fair amount of it too. But David the king could dance, he danced with wild abandon, he danced as if no one were watching. He found joy in his vocation, and was not afraid to show it. Pick a vocation, live a life, that makes your soul dance.

Chapter Twenty-Two

DON'T MARRY A ROCK

*You may ask whether ordinary human beings
ever seriously and perseveringly transcend themselves.
I think they do so when they fall in love.
Then their being becomes being-in-love.
Such being-in-love has its antecedents,
its causes, conditions, its occasions.
But once it has occurred and as long as it lasts,
it takes over.
It becomes the first principle.
From it flows one's desires and fears,
one's joys and sorrows,
one's discernment of values,
one's vision of possibilities,
one's decisions and deeds.*

Bernard Lonergan, SJ

Andy and Leslie were high school sweethearts. Actually they go further back; Leslie remembers when she first met Andy, a tall sinewy blond athlete. He doesn't remember meeting her at all. On the surface they had nothing in common other than the color of their hair.

He was tall, she was short; she was expressive, he was stoic; she an artist, he a jock; he excelled at math and science, she excelled in liberal arts; but sooner or later Andy did notice Leslie and something stuck. They dated through high school and when Andy received an out-of-state athletic scholarship, Leslie decided to go to the same university. That's where I first met them—met Leslie, I mean, faithfully sitting in the stands, sitting there when it rained, sitting there when the sun blistered the field, sitting there in the early snow, sitting there watching Andy play, sitting there when he was injured and couldn't play. They would walk campus hand in hand, his head inclining down to hers reaching up. That's how they were in church; that's how I remember them.

To no one's surprise, they were to be married. They snuck letters of gratitude to their parents into the wedding program. In addition to all the usual things you might thank parents for, they thanked them for the times they saw their parents sneak into the hallway and kiss when they thought no one was looking, for the times when one did the dishes for the other, or rubbed each other's feet when tired, or just let the other fall asleep on the couch, or watch uninterrupted their favorite program. They thanked them because after a long week of work, their parents would wake up early on precious weekend mornings to drive a hoard of smelly grumpy boys an unbelievable distance so they could play a tournament, or go to a practice, or watch someone famous play. They thanked them for sacrificing time and money for equipment, entry fees, and endlessly feeding a voracious team just because their son was on it. They thanked them because these are the moments that taught them what love was, and when they found themselves sacrificing for each other as they had seen their parents do, they knew they were ready to be married.

A sweet gesture, yes, but incredibly wise insight; they learned from their parents how to let someone else's agenda, someone's needs shape their own life. Way beyond opposites attracting, Leslie and Andy's love was built by each allowing each other to influence, shape, and mold their lives. It wasn't a matter of tolerating each other's differences; it was a matter of embracing them, each becoming an evolutionary force in the life of the other. And so they have remained happily married: tending, shaping each other's lives, now allowing their four children to add unexpected surprise and challenge.

If you want to marry someone who is going to be just the same thirty years later as the day you met them, then you should marry a rock. If you want to be exactly the same person you are now in thirty years, then you want to be a rock. The vocation of marriage is an invitation to change, an invitation to be mutually vulnerable to changes you will produce in each other. It is quite a thing, to spend your one wild and precious life creating and confronting change together.

Chapter Twenty-Three

DON'T MARRY THE PERFECT PERSON

*To welcome imperfection is to accept friendship
as an unfinished history,
one that includes ourselves actively in the retelling.
In imperfection, it is always possible
to begin and begin again.*

Fr. Tolentino

Somewhere in the world is the one perfect person God has planned for you to marry. One person, exactly designed for you, like a piece of the puzzle that fits only one other piece, is waiting for you to find them. When you meet, you will know, it will be obvious, and then, you will be happy. This is nonsense. God has not planned your love life like a scavenger hunt. Unless you find all the requisite pieces you lose. To think that you were born in Kansas City and God placed the person you were meant to marry in Mumbai, and unless you find them you are screwed, is to mistake the God of Jesus Christ for a cruel trickster pagan god. To think that you are such an intricate and delicate creature that you can fall in love and marry one and only one other person is to sell yourself way short.

You can and will love many people. What makes the love you will share with the person you marry is that you both choose your love: pledge yourself to honor and defend it, forsaking all others, until death do you part. There may be others with whom you are more compatible, others with whom you have a "better fit." What makes your love special is that you choose it, you choose each other not because you are perfect for each other, but because you love each other.

I knew Steve and Mary when they first met. Their attraction was immediate, exciting, and passionate. Bursting with curiosity about each other, they easily talked long into the night, found pleasure in each other's company and shared joy. They had, as couples do, ups and downs, but well within normal limits. Time passed, years actually, six, maybe seven. I had since moved and was not up to date on all things Steve and Mary. The sand slipping through the hourglass gave me doubts about their future together. The phone rang (we still had phones in those days) with Steve announcing that he and Mary were going to be married. *"Not all at once, but slowly, over the years, little by little,"* he explained, *"I showed her all the bad parts of me. There is nothing left, nothing she doesn't know, there is nothing left to hide. She still loves me. That's how I know I should marry her."*

Steve is a wise man, and a loving one. In the Garden of Eden, Adam and Eve were naked and unashamed. They trusted each other because they had nothing to hide. Their love wasn't motivated by mutual perfection; it was based on mutual forgiveness. *"Love is patient; love is kind; love is not envious or boastful or arrogant or rude. It does not insist on its own way; it is not irritable or resentful; it does not rejoice in wrongdoing, but rejoices in the truth. It bears all things, believes all things, hopes all things, endures all things. Love never ends."* This is a formula for mercy, not perfection.

If marriage is your vocation, don't wait for the perfect

person. Look for the person you want to know for the rest of your life. Look for the person who wants to know you, all of you, the good and the bad. When the two of you can be naked and unashamed, when you are both eager to bathe each other's faults with mercy for the rest of your lives, then get married. You have found your mutual vocation. You have found the person who will show you the face of God.

Chapter Twenty-Four

HOLINESS IS VISIBLE

To have and to hold, from this day forward, for better, for worse, for richer, for poorer, in sickness and in health, to love and to cherish, till death do us part.

*M*arriage vows are exchanged once, but repeated many times. I learned this while flying into Savannah to spend some time with my sister on Hilton Head Island. July being what it is in the deep South, thunderstorms delayed my flight just long enough to get everyone cranky. I realized everyone's plane was delayed when a mob surrounded the car rental desk. It's an hour's drive to Hilton Head. The rental line was as long as the flight, which improved no one's mood. Standing in line, trying to be polite and avoid mortal sin, I caught sight of one couple in the line next to me. The man was tall, thin white legs poking out of Bermuda shorts that did not match the wrinkled Hawaiian shirt and bedraggled straw hat. He was looking down at his wife, a woman who maybe reached halfway up his chest. She was wearing deep green shorts and a pink shirt, with pudgy legs swelling out of her sandals. She reminded me of a watermelon. She was facing him and complaining in a ringing voice: they were stuck on the runway, the flight was bumpy. They only served peanuts; and now the lines were long. Her feet hurt, and they were going to be late checking into their time-share. If she were two years old she would have thrown back her head, screaming and wailing her misery.

He just stood there, looking down so he could see into her eyes. He was intently listening, so as to not miss a word she said, although everyone in the airport could hear every word just fine. He mumbled a few words urging her to be patient, telling her it would be alright—but this only agitated her, so he stopped talking.

Never taking his eyes off her, his white bony hand reached up and started stroking and rearranging her hair. She had the sort of hair you have when you are just starting or just recovering from chemotherapy. It was stringy and multi-colored, just strands really over her bald head. Her hairs were sweaty and they stuck together and pasted themselves on her scalp. His fingers were stroking and rearranging her hairs so they went from front to back.

"You are beautiful," he softly drawled. *"You are beautiful darling, so beautiful, beautiful."* Never taking his eyes from hers he spoke so softly no one could hear him for her complaining. But she heard him. Throwing her gesticulating arms around his waist, pressing her face into his chest in sweaty hug, all her fears, tiredness, and insecurity pressed into him. He threw his scrawny arm around her shoulders, kissed the top of her balding head, his bony hand still arranging her hair as he repeated his drawl, *"You are beautiful, you are beautiful darling, so beautiful, beautiful."*

Tears came to my eyes. *How much he loves her*, I thought to myself.

Tears came because it was so tender. Tears came because I was jealous; I wanted someone to love me like that to stroke away my burdens and frustration.

Tears came because I wondered if I ever loved anyone as much as this man loved this woman. Tears came because I had just heard the still small voice of the God of love whispering in the lobby of National Car Rental.

We expect the voice of God to be pyrotechnics: the thunder, firebolt, earthquake, and whirlwind that demands our attention and cannot be avoided. We expect that God will produce special effects that exceed the noises and miracles we produce on our own. While God can do all that, he seldom does. The voice of God is often whispered by one spouse into the ear of the other: whispered by someone who looks at our antics and sees only our needs. It is not just their voice whispering to us, theirs is the voice of God, heard not in spectacle but in quiet moments. These are the special voices shared between married couples. In the life of a successful marriage, couples exchange vows of love in many forms. If God's still small voice can happen in an airport lobby, it can happen anywhere, on the subway, on the street, in the kitchen, the car, the bedroom. Couples whisper God's voice to each other even when one of them feels they are drowning, whispering, *"You are beautiful. I am here with you, and I am going to hold you. You are not alone; we'll get through this together."*

Chapter Twenty-Five

RELIGIOUS LIFE

A Religious Order is an evidence of an uncommon or special grace given to a certain number of souls, so that they may be sanctified by the practice of particular virtues to meet the spiritual needs of their epoch, and in this way to renew the spiritual life of the members of the church and to extend her fold.

Servant of God, Isaac Thomas Hecker, CSP

Throughout Christian history women and men have banded together to form communities whose purpose is to develop the spiritual lives of their members for the good of the universal church. These women and men fulfill their individual vocation by living and working within these communities. Religious communities usually have a founder, whose individual gift or charism permeates the community. The members of the community carry on the charism of the founder, living lives according to a "rule" or tradition established by the founder, which most commonly included some version of vows or promises of poverty, chastity, and obedience. Some of these communities are contemplative—their major purpose is to pray and develop a deep interior spiritual life within a cloistered religious community they will never leave. Some communities are primarily apostolic: they bond together in common life for the fulfillment of a mission for the church.

Religious communities are self-governing; they elect their own leadership. Some have a distinctive way of dress (habit); others dress in simple ordinary clothes anyone would wear. Many follow a spiritual life patterned after their founder.

Throughout time, religious communities pop up to meet specific needs of the church. As time passes some communities adapt their origins to the evolving needs of the church, while others, having served the purpose God intended, fade away. Among male religious orders, some members may be priests, while others are not ordained and live as "brothers." Religious orders of women have supplied the church with special genius and spiritual skill. In the Catholic tradition, women and men vow to live the rest of their lives in the community they join. Pope Francis, for example, is a member of the Society of Jesus, or as they are more commonly known, the Jesuits. Even though he is the pope, he continues to be a Jesuit.

As you pursue your vocation and think about whether you are called to a specific form of religious life, you may find yourself wanting to live and work with others rather than by yourself. You may feel called to live a particular way of life, or dedicate yourself to a single mission. That doesn't make you weird; it simply means that maybe you are called to be part of this ancient tradition of living the common religious life. In the United States alone there are more than forty-nine thousand religious women, twelve thousand religious priests, and four thousand religious brothers. A recent analysis of people entering religious life characterized them in the following way: *The data show that those who do so tend to be optimistic, well educated, have held real jobs in the real world, and are not afraid of authority. They look to live with other optimistic people who possess a strong Catholic identity and are people of hope. They want to live in community and share a common prayer life."*

If this sounds like you, it is time to check out different forms of religious life. Go online and look for VISION Resources, part of the Vision Vocation Network (https://vocationnetwork.org). There you can explore hundreds of religious communities, find vocation resources, and even take an online vocation match survey that will pair you with religious communities who might be a good fit for you. Religious orders of women and men have supplied the church with diverse radical and unique forms of spiritual and pastoral creativity. Don't be afraid to think that you might find your vocation in that exciting tradition.

Chapter Twenty-Six

THINKING ABOUT PRIESTHOOD

To the full extent of my power,
because I am a priest,
I wish from now on to be the first
to become conscious of all
that the world loves, pursues, and suffers;
the first to seek, to sympathize and to suffer;
the first to open myself out and sacrifice myself—
to become more widely human and
more nobly of the earth
than any of the world's servants.

Pierre Teilhard de Chardin

If you are thinking of being a priest, you are not crazy; you may in fact be called. These days people don't come to the idea of priesthood all on their own; God either puts the idea in your head or asks someone else to put the idea in your head. God isn't calling you to the priesthood to punish you, to deprive you of what everybody has. God isn't calling you to the priesthood because you are better than anyone else. God is calling you to the priesthood because this is the best way to live your one wild, precious life. God is calling you to the priesthood to love the world for Christ's sake.

Why should you think about being a priest? Let me tell you. All Christians are baptized priests, prophets, and kings, but the word of God drifts away from the best of us, grows faint in our hearing, undecipherable, seemingly irrelevant to life as we are forced to live it. So we need priests to kindle the word of God in our hearts. We need priests to huff and puff on the dying embers of our souls so once again God's flame burns within us.

Christians believe in the presence of God. God is everywhere, the Creator of heaven and earth and you, but the best of us lose sight of him and can forget what God's touch feels like. So we need priests not just to jog our memories of God but to make God's love present again, really present, most of all in the Eucharist, where we see him, and in his memory eat his body and drink his blood, and become all together his Mystical Body.

We need priests in baptism and confirmation to celebrate and strengthen life. We need priests in confession to whisper God's mercy to souls who have forgotten it is possible.

We need priests in marriage to bless loves that have blessed each other; and we need priests in our illness, and again at our death to remind us that the gentle hands of God are a good place to take our rest.

There is a lot of noise out there; voices shouting, screaming, the devil ever busy separating one of us from the other, encouraging us to fight as if there were not enough love to go around. Evil defeats us, discourages us, and even seduces us.

So we need priests to strengthen knees that have become weak and hands grown weary of building the kingdom of God: the kingdom to which all are welcome, all loved. This kingdom is where peace is built with justice and mercy. This kingdom is the place where the poor and those on the periph-ery have places of honor.

Christians have all been baptized priest, prophet, and king; but we need priestly service. We need priests to help us live our vocations, whatever they are. We need priests to encourage us to live with our own wild and precious life.

So think about it. Think if God is calling you to live the wild, wonderful, precious life of a priest.

Chapter Twenty-Seven

GOING TO SEMINARY

"Do you know him to be worthy?"
"After inquiry among the Christian people,
and upon the recommendation of those responsible,
I testify that he has been found worthy."
"Relying on the help of the Lord our God and our
Savior Jesus Christ, we chose our brother
for the order of priesthood."

Ordination Rite

You cannot figure whether God is calling you to be a priest on your own. You don't own the call to priesthood; you have to be called to the priesthood by the church, by the people of God, whom you will serve. You will have lots of help in deciding whether or not you should be a priest. This takes a lot of pressure off your shoulders. You are not right away making a decision to be a priest; you are actually making a decision to check it out and see if it is for you. You are making a decision to go to a seminary, which is different from making your final decision to answer God's call to be a priest. Going to the seminary is not jumping off a cliff; it is beginning a journey into your soul.

You don't flunk out of seminary like you flunk out of boot camp. A decision is reached that priesthood either is or is not the best way to live your life. Twenty-one men started in my first year, thirteen went on to the second year, and finally six of us were ordained. I believe in my heart of hearts that each one of us came for as long as we should have. Being in the seminary, even if they didn't finish, was an important part of each person's journey to their true vocation. It was part of how they and God were working out who they should be and how they should do it. Those of us who were called to ordination are not the ones "who made it." We all made it, ordained or not; we all found our true vocation. So don't freak out about your decision to go to seminary. Your time there will not be wasted. It may be, even if just for a short time, the place where you must be to have a conversation with God.

So just how does seminary help you discern whether you are called to priesthood? Seminary is more than studying the-ology and learning to administer the rites of the church. It is where you begin to live the life you wonder if God is calling you to live. Saint Frances de Sales wasn't thinking of semi-nary when he wrote this, he wrote this for everyone, but I think it also applies to seminary:

> There are many who want me to tell them of secret ways of becoming perfect and I can only tell them that the sole secret is a hearty love of God, and the only way of attaining that love is by loving. You learn to speak by speaking, to study by studying, to run by running, to work by working; and just so you learn to love God and man by loving. Begin as a mere apprentice and the very power of love will lead you on to become a master of the art.

In seminary you gradually begin to live the life of a priest, and as you do, discover whether this is the way you are called to love. It is here you discover whether you can live a celibate lifestyle with integrity, whether you can live a life of priestly service, whether you believe what the church believes, can teach what you believe, and practice what you preach.

Don't get me wrong: seminary is not easy, and the path is not always clear. I was the world's worst seminarian, a significant challenge for my formation team, to say nothing of God. But for me, the seminary discernment process worked. I entered thinking I was doing God a favor. I was going to save the world and the church and my religious order. I left the seminary with the humble realization that priesthood was how God was going to save me.

Chapter Twenty-Eight

RELIGIOUS WOMEN

Christ has no body now but yours.
No hands, no feet on earth but yours.
Yours are the eyes through which he
looks compassion on this world.
Yours are the feet with which he walks to do good.
Yours are the hands through which
he blesses all the world.
Yours are the hands, yours are the feet,
yours are the eyes, you are his body.
Christ has no body now on earth but yours.

St. Teresa of Avila

The church in the United States was built and sustained by religious women. By church I mean the believing church, the working church. The church composed of women, men, and children who love God and love their neighbor; the men and women who live lives of faith, hope, and love; the men and women who pray for victims of injustice and work to make justice a living, breathing reality. Bishops, priests, brothers have played their part, but when push comes to shove, religious women have been the "boots on the ground," teaching by word and example what it is written in Scripture:

"Little children, let us love, not in word or speech, but in truth and action."

Catholic immigrant children were educated by religious women. They were prepared for the sacraments by religious women. They learned of the love of God from religious women. When they were sick, they were treated in hospitals established and run by religious women. When women were not welcomed at places of higher education, religious women founded colleges to enable women to have the same access to higher education as did men. People abused by slumlords were ministered to by religious women who also fought for their right to decent housing. Religious women worked and suffered for the civil rights of Native Americans and African Americans. The "Nuns on the Bus" are part of a long tradition of loving, determined religious women who are not content to allow the poor to suffer in silence. When the Second Vatican Council called for a renewal of religious life according to the charism of their founder, religious women led the way. Women religious are now among the most learned theological minds and voices in the world. Religious women were among the first to point out clerical sexual abuse and insist on action to protect children and punish perpetrators. Contemplative orders of religious women sustain a needy church with the sheer power of their prayer.

I want to be clear about this, because if you are a woman thinking about religious life you are not crazy. You may be called to one of the most generous and essential vocations in the church. The first thing you should do if this has entered your mind is to contact a woman in committed religious life and talk with her, or talk with several religious women. I promise you will discover in them a ready, wise, and compassionate ear, and a genuinely holy, brave soul to guide you.

Chapter Twenty-Nine

BELONGING

The two most important days in your life
are the day you are born and
the day you find out why.

Mark Twain

The contemporary answer to the question of the meaning of life, and what our role in life is, derives from what we achieve and what we acquire. Pecking order and possessions are all there is to deciphering meaning and purpose. For the religious person, identity and meaning do not come from achievement and acquisition, but from belonging, belonging to God.

The Bible is a book of belonging. Who am I? I am one of God's people: God's chosen, precious in God's eyes. What makes me important? I am important because I am the beloved of God, who made heaven and earth. What is the purpose of my life? To be faithful to the God who is faithful to me; to love the One who loves me, as Jesus says, with all my heart, my mind, and all my strength. Cardinal Reinhold Marx, the archbishop of Munich, says it this way:

> Many older people have grown up with the idea that the church is a moral institution and that God is only a merciful God if we keep his commandments.

But God doesn't say, "If you're good, then I'll also be good to you." Jesus proclaims a God who says, "I love you—so live," and thus gives us the freedom to decide whether we want to accept and return his love.

Faith is not intellectual conviction in a set of abstract dogmas; faith is a decision to accept the invitation to belong to God. Belong not in the sense of a piece of property, but belong as a matter of fit, belonging because you are entitled to be there. *"Home,"* Robert Frost wrote, *"is the place where, when you have to go there, they have to take you in...something you somehow haven't to deserve."* That is what it is like to belong to God.

Jesus also tells us that this process of me belonging to God also involves me belonging to you and you belonging to me: being faithful to one another, loving each other with all our heart, our mind, and our strength. Because we do not love each other this way, because we are not faithful to each other with all our heart and mind and strength, our belonging breaks down into factions. Our world is divided into those I love, those like me, those unlike me, those I hate, those I ignore.

This is why I want you to give serious thought to making at least part of your vocation belonging to the church. By church, I mean the Risen Body of Christ through which Jesus comes into a broken reality where we belong to no one but ourselves to re-educate us to God's reality of belonging to love with all of our heart, our mind, and our strength. The church is where faith is lived as union and communion, with God and with each other. It is the place that preserves and passes on God's love lessons through the Bible and the lived experience of the church.

How does that actually work? Let's start with page 1 of God's love lessons, found in the Book of Exodus, which reads,

"You shall not wrong or oppress a resident alien....You shall not abuse any widow or orphan....If you lend money to my people, to the poor among you, you shall not deal with them as a creditor; you shall not exact interest from them." These basic standards for belonging to one another are the requirements for belonging to God. I am intrigued however by the basis for them: *"You shall not wrong or oppress a resident alien, for you were aliens in the land of Egypt."* Remember, you once were in need of help. Remember, there was a time when you were down. Remember, there was a time when you needed mercy. Remember, there was a time when you were in their shoes. The biblical basis for belonging is empathy with the one in need.

Since empathy is foundational in Scripture, it is worth thinking about how it develops in us. Psychologists believe that we are biologically hardwired to develop empathy. Shared feeling is the most basic level of empathy. You have seen a group of birds feeding: one spies a cat and one flies off, then all the others do as well. All the other birds feel the fear of the bird that flew away, are now alarmed, and, flying away, are now safe.

The second level of empathic development is not a group experience but is seen when someone notices the distress or pain of another. Seeing someone else in pain, we are reminded of our own experience of pain and respond to them as we wish someone would respond to us. On the toddler's playground little Susie sees little Johnny crying so Susie brings her own mother to care for Johnny. Susie knows what it is like to cry. She knows her mother cares for her, so she brings her mother to care for Johnny. The next level of empathic development is when we see someone in need and then go outside of ourselves and our experience to discover what will relieve their need. Little Susie sees little Johnny crying. And then she runs to bring Johnny not to her mother but Johnny's mother.

This higher level of response comes when we feel the distress of another strongly enough to respond to it, but respond to that person not on the basis of what we would need but on the basis of what they need.

This is a level of belonging that calls me out of myself and into the world of another. This is a level of belonging that teaches me that my experience of the world is not the only one there is. This is a level of belonging that teaches me to look for my identity and meaning outside of myself, to look to God and to look toward others with all my heart, all my soul, all my mind.

Love, Jesus teaches us, is the greatest commandment. Love commands me to get out of my life into your life. This is how love changes me: love commands me to get out of my life and into the lives of the widow, the orphan, the alien, immigrant, and homeless, the oppressed and the needy. Love commands me to get out of my life and into the lives of those who surround me every day. People I take for granted, people I never notice, people I do not want to notice.

Love commands me to find my identity and my meaning by belonging with all my heart, all my soul, all my mind to others, and when I do that, then I will have found my identity, value, and meaning in belonging to God, in loving God, with all my heart, all my soul, and all my mind. This is hard to do all on your own. So give some thought to belonging to the church, whose faith is all about belonging.

Chapter Thirty

BURDENS

*The first rule of the Christian missionary is:
Nothing needs correcting as much
as other people's habits.*

Mark Twain

When many people think of religion, the first thing they think of is other people telling them how to live, laying burdens on their shoulders, correcting their behavior, scolding their desires, sprinkling their souls with guilt and remorse. Traditionally, religious people have a keen eye for fault, and let's face it, the world provides a lot of fault to observe.

One of the things that has always drawn me to Jesus is his ability to see other people, to see past their social façade and public mask, to see even past their obvious sins, and see the burdens they really carry. You and I come and we go, carrying burdens that no one sees. When asked how we are, we all say we are doing fine. That is a big lie. What we mean is that we are keeping our burdens to ourselves, maybe because we have learned that the other person doesn't really want to hear about our burdens, and even if they knew, they wouldn't lift a finger to help us anyway. So what is the point?

In my imagination, I have a picture in my mind that

when we die and are in line to get into heaven, we will be shocked—shocked because we will see for the first time all the burdens each person is carrying. Mark my words, each person there will be laden down—bent over double, some of them—with the burdens of their lives. Some we might have known were there, or we could have guessed, but most of them will be completely unknown to us. Some people will be carrying burdens they didn't even know about. Each day, like it or not, know it or not, people carry their burdens like too much luggage at the airport or on the subway: trying to push it along, struggling to carry what they really can't.

But if we are waiting in line to get into heaven, when we finally can see the burdens other people carry, we will all take turns helping each other with each other's "luggage" until we reach the gate, where in my dream, Jesus, as the sacred "redcap," takes the burdens off our shoulders so we can walk freely into God's presence. That is my vision of purgatory, the place where we finally see all the burdens everyone around us is carrying: the place where we each carry some of the load others carry so that they can reach Jesus, who will take the burden off their shoulders forever.

Well, purgatory may or may not be like that, but one thing is sure: Jesus believes that religion should be like that. Religion as a community of shared faith should be the place where we learn to see all the burdens carried by the people around us, and seeing those burdens, help that person carry their load to Jesus who can set them free.

Burdens come in all shapes and sizes. We carry individual psychological, emotional, spiritual, and relationship burdens. Employers and employees carry burdens. Many do not have safe or affordable housing. Everyone needs to compete to just hold a job capable of providing for a family, educate our young, purchase health care, and secure a dignified retirement. Sickness, acute and chronic, weighs heavily on people's shoulders. External burdens are imposed by prejudice, racism, and economic exploitation. We have the ever-increasing burden of caring for an environment that can be damaged beyond repair—a burden that seems beyond our individual control. Some of you will embrace vocations that operate at a macrolevel, while others focus on a more interpersonal level. No matter your individual vocation, your vocation as a Christian is not about burdening people with your judgements, it is about heavy lifting, and that is why you are needed in the church. Jesus needed Simon of Cyrene to help him carry his cross, and the Risen Lord needs you in his church to help him carry the world's cross.

Chapter Thirty-One

WHY NOT BE A SAINT?

"Who are these, robed in white,
and where have they come from?"
I said to him, "Sir, you are the one that knows."
Then he said to me, "These are they who have come
out of the great ordeal; they have washed their robes
and made them white in the blood of the Lamb."

Revelation

No matter what vocation is yours, regardless of your career or aptitude, regardless of how religious you are, I want you to give serious consideration to becoming a saint. We are surrounded by the saints. Saints come in handy. To begin, they remind you that you do not "have a soul," you are a soul, what you have is a body. Saints remind you that you are not a lonely little soul making your way through the universe in isolation. You are part of a vast procession of souls, souls that from the very beginning of time are on a journey to the God of love. The Book of Revelation paints a picture of all these souls finally assembled on the last day of time, and describes them as *"these are they who have come out of the great ordeal; they have washed their robes and made them white in the blood of the Lamb."* What a vivid contradictory image: *"To wash something clean in blood."*

The garments they have washed are their lives. The blood they have washed them in is the sacrificial love of Jesus Christ, the Lamb of God who takes away the sin of the world.

During the journey that is their lives, they have immersed themselves in love of Jesus: that sacrificial love of Jesus that pours itself out for their families, their friends, their lovers; for those they met who suffer, for the poor, for those who could not defend or provide for themselves, for the cause of knowledge and truth, for justice, for the preservation of the planet. In the course of their life, these souls had trials during which they had to make choices, choices for or against all of this. These souls, these saints, chose to walk in the way of love. They have formed a procession of love and you follow right behind, in their footsteps. You are in the footsteps of the saints, not just the great saints like Paul, but all those unknown and unnamed saints whose love is not less because they are anonymous.

I read a *New York Times* article entitled, *"Young Migrants Reach Europe Alone, Abused and Afraid."* The article told the harrowing stories of immigrant children, like Reza Mohammed, a seven-year-old boy refugee lost in a Serbian forest. Legs caked in mud, he lost track of his family and sat down on a tree stump until they found him. They never did. Who found him was a stranger, a man from the same part of Afghanistan as the boy's family. Realizing the boy was not safe from the police or predators, the man took Reza by the hand and journeyed with him to Germany, where the boy now lives in a home run by nuns. The article went on to describe other children, one story worse than the other. The stories of boys desperately escaping recruitment as child soldiers or suicide bombers. Some of these boys have never held a coloring pen in their hand, but had seen their own father beheaded. It told the stories of girls who reported such sadistic sexual violence that their German youth worker said, *"We did not have the words*" to include the details in her report. There were Syrian children rescued from a boat that sank in the Mediterranean who saw their friends drown before their eyes.

The article ended hopefully:

> Little Reza has made progress, his caregiver said, he attends a regular primary school, the crayons in his pencil case are neatly organized by color, "already more German than German," and sometimes he falls asleep without crying.

My point is this: the soldier who found him in the woods is a saint to Reza. The German nuns who care for him and helped him find his family are saints to Reza. Those who listen to their unspeakable stories of tragedy are saints to the children who must tell them. Those who quietly sit along bedsides are saints to the children who cry themselves to sleep. Throughout our lives people have been saints to us. Their faces are not on holy cards, no churches are named after them. We may not even remember their names, but they have been saints to us. Now is your time, your journey, your great time of trial, your time to choose sacrificial love, your time to be a saint for others. Be a saint, even if you can only do so for a moment, even if your sainthood is too heavy a burden to continually carry.

Be a saint, not just for yourself, and not just for those whose lives will be touched with your love. You are not the end point in the procession of souls; choose to be a saint for all those who will follow where you will lead, lead them in the procession of all the saints, in procession toward the God of love.

Chapter Thirty-Two

FAILURE

A certain young man was following him,
wearing nothing but a linen cloth.
They caught hold of him, but he left the
linen cloth and ran off naked.

Mark

I was named after the streaker in the Garden of Gethsemane, who tradition associates with the writer of the Gospel of Mark. Just a few hours ago, he was with the followers of Jesus, who promised that they would die defending him, and when push came to shove, ran naked into the night just to get away from him. Failure distinguishes all of Jesus's followers, and is nakedly featured to encourage later generations of Christians who experience failure all on their own. If the earliest followers of Jesus, those who lived with him, heard his voice, ate and drank with him, traveled with him—if they failed him, then maybe there is some hope for the rest of us. Hope, not because we are better than they are, but hope because they overcame their failures to spread the story of Jesus the world over.

Failure is going to be part of your vocation story, as it is part of everyone else's vocation story. In his first interview, Pope Francis, when asked, *"Who is Jorge Mario Bergoglio?"*

replied, *"I am a sinner."* If Pope Francis freely acknowledges his mistakes, then the rest of us can as well. I even want to go a step further and suggest that failure is an essential part of our vocation, so learning to deal with failure is essential to having a successful life. I am going to suggest three keys to thinking about failure.

The first and most obvious key to understanding failure is as the path to success. The ancient Greeks encouraged athletes to always compete against better athletes. The theory was that you can learn only from people who are better than you. If you don't get freaked out by losing and are humble enough to learn why and how someone is better, then you cannot only improve your own skills, you can learn how to stay calm in pressured situations. The best basketball player of my time was the legendary Michael Jordan, who was quoted as saying, *"I've missed more than 9000 shots in my career. I've lost almost 300 games. 26 times, I've been trusted to take the game winning shot and missed. I've failed over and over and over again in my life. And that is why I succeed."* The key is to have the humility and determination to do more than be discouraged from failure, and learn from it.

Second, failure gives perspective. Human beings have always envisioned themselves as potential gods. The Greeks were always trying to steal from the gods, Adam and Eve were trying to eat from the tree of knowledge that would make them like God, and if we are to tell the truth, even devoted religiously motivated people are prone to perfectionism. It is a subtle type of pride that expects that they will achieve perfection, developing a messianic sense of self-importance. If they do not achieve that exalted state, they are ruthless self-critics, and can be fanatical critics of others. When I find myself building the kingdom of God single-handedly, it does me good to remember these words:

Unless the LORD *builds the house,*
those who build it labor in vain.
Unless the LORD *guards the city,*
the guard keeps watch in vain.
It is in vain that you rise up early
and go late to rest,
eating the bread of anxious toil;
for he gives sleep to his beloved. (Psalm 127)

Third, failure is an occasion for mercy. The monk Thomas Merton reflected that in the early part of his life, he believed that saints were people who focused all their energies on being better than other people, surpassing the average person in prayer, virtue, and holiness. Over the course of his life, he learned that saints didn't see themselves as better than other people. True saints see themselves as exactly like all other people, and see how, like all other people, they need the mercy of God. My young naked ancestor eventually wove his way through the trees of Gethsemane, and in the night made his way back to the upper room, making his way back to Jesus. It was Mark, who needed the mercy of Jesus, who wrote the Gospel that brings the mercy of Jesus to the rest of us. You never know how God will use your failures to bring you to your vocation.

Chapter Thirty-Three

JOURNEY, NOT DESTINATION

Two roads diverged in a yellow wood,
And sorry I could not travel both
And be one traveler

Robert Frost

So you make a choice, you think you understand your vocation, and you are banging on with your life. The thought crosses your mind, a whisper at first—scarcely heard, easily dismissed—could I be doing something else? The whisper becomes a chant, impossible to ignore: there were lots of options you never even thought of when you were making your decision. People and opportunities are everywhere you look: Should you be with someone else, should you do something else, could you be someone else?

Sometimes the choice isn't yours; you intended to spend your life one way and now you can't. The person you intended to be with broke up with you. The market has changed and the career you prepared for no longer exists, not for you anyway. The cost of living makes it impossible to stay where you always wanted to live.

Life happens, you understand that, but shouldn't God have clued you in? I mean, *"you knit me together in my mother's womb"* and all those other Bible verses about God knowing us, would it have been so terrible for God to tell you to wait an extra few years for the right person, job, opportunity? Or if you are on the right track, a little signal of divine confidence would be appreciated. Moses had pillars of fire and smoke to guide him—what is wrong with sending you a small sign now and again? Why doesn't life come with a heavenly GPS?

I know it doesn't make you feel better but this is pretty normal reaction. There is even a prayer about it, written by the Trappist monk, Thomas Merton:

> My Lord God, I have no idea where I am going. I do not see the road ahead of me. I cannot know for certain where it will end. Nor do I really know myself, and the fact that I think that I am following your will does not mean that I am actually doing so. But I believe that the desire to please you does in fact please you. And I hope I have that desire in all that I am doing. I hope that I will never do anything apart from that desire. And I know that if I do this you will lead me by the right road, though I may know nothing about it. Therefore will I trust you always, though I may seem to be lost and in the shadow of death. I will not fear, for you are ever with me, and you will never leave me to face my perils alone.

Your vocation is the story of your life with God. The way you live your life is how you love God with your whole heart, soul, mind, and strength. There are many paths in the woods you can take. What is important is that you make a

94

choice, and with that choice try to please God the best you can. Do that, and there is no road God will not walk with you. Everyone loses confidence from time to time; when that happens to you, remember what the angels always say: the Lord is with you, be not afraid.

Chapter Thirty-Four

GOD MAKES IT UP AS WE GO ALONG

Love does not sit there like a stone;
it has to be made, like bread, remade
all the time, made new.

Ursula Le Guin

These reflections began with me suggesting that God does not have a predetermined plan for your one wild and precious life. What God does plan for your life is to love you. God accompanies you with that love your whole life long. God hopes that you respond to divine love with the love of your own making.

The world in which you and your love happens is an evolutionary one, constantly changing, adapting, developing in reaction to and along with everyone and everything in that world. As you create and recreate your love, God is happy to accompany you, to make up your future wherever you go along together. Take a wrong road, experience a frustrated hope, suffer an abject failure, God will be there crafting and recrafting your vocation with you. There is no place you can go where God won't find you. There is nothing you can do to make God love you less. There is nothing you can do to make God love you more than God already does right now. No matter how unhospitable the environment that surrounds you, the basic ingredients of your vocation are already within you. Jesus is your guide to crafting the best possible love you can be, the Holy Spirit is the fire within, and the church, the people of God who struggle to live and love and believe, will support you if you give them a chance.

Be wild! Don't be afraid to take the risks love and creativity demand, remembering that no matter what message despair whispers in your ear, there is no failure from which you cannot recover. God has lots of practice working with human mistakes. Your vocation is not static, it is constantly adapting to life. If this seems indefinite and insecure, well, good vocations often feel that way. Pope Francis says that he used to think faith was a beacon on a hill providing a clear, bright direction, easily seen. He now thinks faith is more like a lamp you hold in the dark, providing you just enough light to take the next step, and the one after that. You simply need enough faith to take your next step.

Precious is who you are in the eyes of God. That is where you begin, and nothing anybody can do will ever change that. So be free to explore, experiment, fail; be daring, bold, even a little reckless in the development and sharing of your gifts. Wild and reckless may sound like unusual spiritual advice until you remember that Gospel story where Jesus felt that to be true to himself he had to go to Jerusalem at Passover—a dangerous place for him. Peter wisely counseled Jesus to be cautious: to avoid an unpredictable environment, to be safe rather than sorry. This friendly advice was recognized by Jesus as the whispers of Satan once again tempting Jesus to not risk love. Jesus bellows, *"Get behind me, Satan"* to counsel that involves hiding yourself, stifling the Spirit within you. The virtue of prudence is making the right decision, taking the right action at the right time. These decisions often look to other people as wild and reckless, and sometimes they are, but sometimes your soul has no other choice.

Prayer is the oxygen of every vocation, and I close with a prayer from the great American Catholic writer, Flannery O'Conner—I hope you make it your own:

> I am so weak God has given me everything, all the tools, instructions for their use, even a good brain to use them, a creative brain to make them immediate for others. God is feeding me and what I am praying for is an appetite. Our Lady of Perpetual Help, pray for me. Amen.

If You Want to Read Some More: Available from Paulist Press

Becoming Who You Are: Insights on the True Self from Thomas Merton and Other Saints, James Martin, SJ

Divine Harmony: Seeking Community in a Broken World, Mary Doak

Faith: Practices, Models and Sources of the Spirit, Cardinal Walter Kasper

Miracle in Motion: Living a Purposeful Life, Antonio Martinez Jr., SJ

No Journey Will Be Too Long: Friendship in Christian Life, José Tolentino Mendonça

Pope Francis Talks to Couples: Wisdom on Marriage and Family, Pope Francis

Sacred Rituals for Every Day, Anselm Grün, OSB

What Are We Doing on Earth for Christ's Sake? Richard Leonard, SJ